AUTORE

Carlo Cucut è nato a Nole (TO) nel 1955. Ha coltivato la passione per la storia sin da ragazzo e negli anni ha approfondito questo interesse dedicandosi alla ricerca storica. Ha pubblicato articoli sulle riviste: "Storia del XX Secolo", "Storie & Battaglie", "Milites" e "Ritterkreuz". In campo editoriale ha pubblicato vari volumi per Marvia Edizioni: "Penne Nere sul confine orientale. Storia del Reggimento Alpini "Tagliamento" 1943-1945", vincitore del Premio De Cia; "Attilio Viziano. Ricordi di un corrispondente di guerra"; "Forze Armate della RSI sul fronte orientale"; "Forze Armate della RSI sul fronte occidentale"; "Forze Armate della RSI sulla linea Gotica"; "Alpini nella Città di Fiume 1944-1945". Per il Gruppo Modellistico Trentino ha pubblicato "Le forze armate della RSI 1943-1945. Forze di terra".

Carlo Cucut was born in Nole (TO) in 1955. He cultivated a passion for history as a boy and over the years has deepened this interest by dedicating himself to historical research. He published articles in the italian magazines: "Storia del XX Secolo", "Storie & Battaglie", "Milites" and "Ritterkreuz". He published various volumes for Marvia Edizioni: "Penne Nere on the eastern border. History of the Alpini's Regiment "Tagliamento" 1943-1945 ", winner of the "De Cia" Award; "Attilio Viziano. Memories of a war correspondent "; "Armed Forces of RSI on the eastern front"; "Armed Forces of RSI on the Western Front"; "Armed Forces of RSI on the Gothic Line"; "Alpini in the City of Rijeka 1944-1945". For the Trentino Modeling Group he published "The armed forces of RSI 1943-1945. Land forces ".

PUBLISHING'S NOTES

None of unpublished images or text of our book may be reproduced in any format without the expressed written permission of Luca Cristini Editore (already Soldiershop.com) when not indicate as marked with license creative commons 3.0 or 4.0. Luca Cristini Editore has made every reasonable effort to locate, contact and acknowledge rights holders and to correctly apply terms and conditions to Content.

Every effort has been made to trace the copyright of all the photographs. If there are unintentional omissions, please contact the publisher in writing at: info@soldiershop.com, who will correct all subsequent editions.

Our trademark: Luca Cristini Editore@, and the names of our series & brand: Soldiershop, Witness to war, Museum book, Bookmoon, Soldiers&Weapons, Battlefield, War in colour, Historical Biographies, Darwin's view, Fabula, Altrastoria, Italia Storica Ebook, Witness To History, Soldiers, Weapons & Uniforms, Storia etc. are herein @ by Luca Cristini Editore.

LICENSES COMMONS

This book may utilize part of material marked with license creative commons 3.0 or 4.0 (CC BY 4.0), (CC BY-ND 4.0), (CC BY-SA 4.0) or (CCo 1.0). We give appropriate attribution credit and indicate if change were made in the acknowledgments field. Our WTW books series utilize only fonts licensed under the SIL Open Font License or other free use license.

For a complete list of Soldiershop titles please contact Luca Cristini Editore on our website: www.soldiershop.com or www.cristinieditore.com. E-mail: info@soldiershop.com

Title: **THE ARTILLERY OF THE ARMED FORCES OF THE ITALIAN SOCIAL REPUBLIC**
Code.: **WTW-018 EN** by Carlo Cucut
ISBN code: 978-88-93276603 first edition November 2020
Text: English Nr. of images: 112 Layoute: 177,8x254mm Cover & Art Design: Luca S. Cristini

WITNESS TO WAR (SOLDIERSHOP) is a trademark of Luca Cristini Editore, via Orio, 35/4 - 24050 Zanica (BG) ITALY.

WITNESS TO WAR

THE ARTILLERY OF THE ARMED FORCES OF THE ITALIAN SOCIAL REPUBLIC

PHOTOS & IMAGES FROM WORLD WARTIME ARCHIVES

CARLO CUCUT

BOOKS TO COLLECT

SUMMARY

Preface...5
Premise...6
Artillery classification...7
Divisional, accompanying artillery and coastal position..8
    Italian artillery...9
        65/17 gun...9
        75/13 Howitzer 9
        75/18 Howitzer 10
        75/27 gun model 906 and model 911..11
        100/17 Howitzer..12
        100/17 Howitzer..13
        105/28 Gun..14
        105/32 Gun..14
        149/13 Howitzer..15
        149/12 Howitzer..15
        149/19 Howitzer..16
        149/35 Gun..17
        210/8 Mortar...17
    Foreign artillery..45
        7,5 cm. le IG 18 (leichte Infanterie Geschutz) Gun..45
        7,5 cm GebG 36 Mountain gun..45
        10,5 cm. le FH 18 (leichte Feld Haubitze) Howitzer...45
        15 cm sIG-33 (15 cm schweres Infanterie Geschütz 1933) Howitzer................................46
        76,2 M1939 Gun...46
        105/27 Gun..47
Anti-tank artillery...48
    Italian artillery...49
        47/32 gun...49
    Foreign artillery..50
        20 mm S anti-tank rifle...50
        Hotchkiss da 25/72 Gun model 34 and model 37...50
        3,7 cm. PaK – 35/36 Gun...51
        45 mm M1937 (53-k) Gun..51
        7,5 cm. PaK 40 Gin...52
Anti-aircraft artillery..65
    Italian artillery...65
        Breda machine gun 20/65 model 35..65
        Scotti-Isotta Fraschini - O.M. 20/70 Machine gun...66
        Breda 37/54 Machine gun..66
        75/46 Gun..67
        76/40 Gun..68
        90/53 Gun..68
    Foreign artillery..70
        20/65 Flak 30–38, FLAKVIERLING..70
        20/70 Oerlikon Machine Gun..70
        Flak-18 da 8,8 cm gun..71
Conclusions..96
Bibliography...97

PREFACE

Among military history enthusiasts, but also among model makers, the study of Italian artillery often appears in second order to topics deemed of greater importance or of greater emotional impact. In recent years this trend has been somewhat reversed and interesting monographs have appeared, dedicated to artillery during the Spanish War and to that of the Royal Army of the Second World War, publications that in part have filled this historiographical gap, but still ample space for an in-depth study of this particular issue for the period after the Armistice, a time span of two years that has not yet been fully studied either on the front of the units of the Social Republic or on that of the so-called departments "Cobelligerants".

For this reason, when Carlo Cucut proposed this to me on a monographic study on the artillery used by the departments of the Italian Social Republic, I immediately thought of proposing it in the "Witness To War" series, knowing for years the expertise with which the author dedicates himself to his personal research. This volume, although conceived with informative intentions, actually covers the topic in an exhaustive manner, with a detailed study of the use of the individual pieces by the most remote departments, allowing enthusiasts to have a complete picture of the use of guns not only by infantry, but also against tank and anti-aircraft, by units of the Army, Navy and Republican National Air Force.

Paolo Crippa

PREMISE

This study intends to fill, or at least try to partially fill, a gap in the artillery equipment present in the Departments of the Armed Forces of the Italian Social Republic.

This is a difficult subject to evaluate since, with the exception of the four Divisions trained in Germany and equipped on the basis of well-defined armament tables, all the Departments that fought under the flag of RSI, did not have a battle order defined by tables. of armament, but they were rather armed with what they had found or recovered during the months of reconstruction.

It is therefore a question of Departments where perhaps only a single piece of artillery was present, statistically insignificant, but essential for the operation of the Department itself and for the task assigned to it.

It should then be added that almost all the war diaries of the individual Departments have been destroyed or dispersed, and the few survivors who have remained many times do not wish to reopen old wounds that have never completely healed.

Here, then, is how, this paper cannot be exhaustive of the subject matter, but only wants to be a starting point from which to begin an in-depth path that can lead to a better result than the one achieved so far.

The authror,

Carlo Cucut

ARTILLERY CLASSIFICATION

Taking up the classification that derives from the use of artillery, we can distinguish:
- Divisional artillery (divided between the various specialties: infantry, mountain, etc.)
- Heavy field artillery of the Army Corps
- Heavy Army artillery
- Anti-aircraft artillery
- Coastal position and position artillery

If these distinctions had value in the context of the Royal Army, structured on Divisions, Corps of the Army, the situation was quite different within the Armed Forces of RSI, where there were four Divisions, on two specialty Regiments and one of Artillery, a Division of the Italian SS, expansion of a Brigade on a ternary structure, the "Decima" Infantry Division of Navy, also structured on a ternary structure, and a significant number of Regiments and Battalions not undivided by the staff and armament very heterogeneous.

Also the Anti-aircraft Artillery (Artiglieria Contraerei or Ar.Co.), which was structured on autonomous groups, and the Coastal Position Artillery Groups were essentially autonomous groups, inserted, the first, within the anti-aircraft defense complex that referred to the structure of Flak Italia, and the latter inserted within the German Fortress Brigades or the Italian Departments.

It is therefore clear that the subdivision of artillery, based on the previously illustrated criterion, cannot have any value if it is included in the reality of the Italian Social Republic.

It was therefore preferred not to follow the rigid logic of the classification, but rather to follow a listing referring to a different cataloging of artillery on the basis of these indications:
- divisional, accompanying artillery from a coastal position
- anti-tank artillery
- anti-aircraft artillery

All this always bearing in mind that what is written is subject to errors and / or omissions and certainly cannot be taken as a final and definitive summary of the matter.

Important Note
In the text, when the number of pieces or batteries is not certain, the question mark (?) has been indicated.

DIVISIONAL, ACCOMPANYING ARTILLERY AND COASTAL POSITION

In this section all the pieces, cannons or howitzers, supplied to the Artillery Regiments of the four Divisions trained in Germany, the Artillery Regiments of the "Decima" Division and the Artillery Regiments of the Italian "SS" Division, in addition to the Artillery Groups have been classified. from Coastal Position and to all those Departments, not undivided, which have in any case used artillery pieces during their operational activity. In some cases, small Departments were reported that had even just one piece of artillery supplied, in other cases, Departments were reported in which it is known that there were pieces but the number is not known.

ITALIAN ARTILLERY

65/17 gun
Adopted in 1911, it began to be distributed to the Departments in 1913. First piece of deformation artillery of the Royal Army designed and built entirely in Italy, it constituted the standard armament of mountain artillery for the duration of World War I. The main flaw of the piece was the reduced Vertical shooting sector, of only 20 ° positive, absolutely insufficient in mountain shooting. After the war it was replaced by the 75/13 howitzer, remaining in service in the field-backed artillery groups. It was heavily used in Abyssinia and Spain. During World War II it was used on all fronts, even as an anti-tank piece, being also installed on trucks or vans, as well as installed in permanent fortifications.

Technical data 65/17 gun
Piece weight in battery: 556 kg
Vertical shooting sector: -7° + 20°
Horizontal shooting sector   : 8°
Grenade weight: 4,2 kg
Initial speed: 348 m/s
Maximum range: 6,5 km, 500 m in antitank shooting

In the Armed Forces of the R.S.I. the 65/17 gun was used by the following units:
- "Italy" Bersaglieri Division: 3 pieces (probably to the Exploring Group)
- "Decima" Navy Infantry Division: "Barbarigo" Battalions - V Company: 4 pieces
- 1st Battery - Autonomous ward located in Opicina (TS): 4 pieces
- The (LI) Bersaglieri Coastal Defense Battalions - deployed to defend Genoa: (?) Pieces
- "Ettore Muti" Mobile Autonomous Legion: 1 piece

75/13 Howitzer
The 75/13 Skoda howitzer has been the regulatory material of the Mountain Artillery Groups for almost 40 years. It was captured in large quantities after the victory of Vittorio Veneto and acquired for war damage repairs from Austria. It was deployed to both mountain artillery groups and a donkey group of infantry divisions and used on all fronts except in Northern Africa.

75/13 howitzers technical data
Piece weight in battery: 613 kg
Vertical shooting sector: -10° + 50°
Horizontal shooting sector: 7°

Grenade weight model 32: 6,3 kg
Initial speed: 378 m/s
Maximum range: 8,2 km

In the Armed Forces of the R.S.I. the 75/13 howitzer was used by the following units:
- 1st "Italy" Bersaglieri Division - 4th Artillery Regiment:
    - The Howitzers Group 3 Batteries: 12 pieces
- 2nd Division Alpini / Grenadiers "Littorio" - 2nd Artillery Regiments:
    - 1st Mountain Group "Gran Sasso": 2 Batteries - 8 pieces
    - 2nd Mountain Group "Romagna": 2 Batteries - 8 pieces
    - 3rd Mountain Group "Verona": 3 Batteries - 12 pieces
- 3rd Infantry Division of Marina "San Marco" - 3rd Artillery Regiment:
    - 1st Group: 3 Batteries - 12 pieces
- 4th "Monterosa" Alpine Division - 1st Artillery Regiment:
    - 1st Group "Aosta": 3 Batteries - 12 pieces
    - 2nd Group "Bergamo": 3 Batteries - 12 pieces
    - 3rd Group "Vicenza": 3 Batteries - 12 pieces
- "Decima" Navy Infantry Division - "Condottieri" Artillery Regiment:
    - "Colleoni" Artillery Group: 1 Battery - 3 pieces
    - "San Giorgio" Artillery Group: 1 Batteries - 4 pieces
    - "Da Giussano" Artillery Group: 2 Batteries - 8 pieces
- 29th Waffen-Grenadier Division der SS - Italienische n.1 - Artillery Regiment: 2 Groups on 2 Batteries each - (?) Pieces
- "Cassanego" Combat Group (Balkans): 5 pieces
- Raggruppamento Anti Partigiani - X Special Artillery Group: 4 Batteries - 16 pieces
- "Cadore" Alpine Battalions - 23rd Battery: 4 pieces
- "Ettore Muti" Mobile Autonomous Legion 2 pieces
- "M" "Venezia Giulia" Cyclist Assault Battalions: 1 Battery - 4 pieces

75/18 Howitzer
The 75/18 model 34 howitzer is the first entirely Italian design and construction campaign deformation model. The piece was presented by Ansaldo in 1932, but was adopted in 1934 and put into production in 1936, with an initial production of only 12 pieces. It was a good piece that was light and easy to simulate, but with a poor range and power. It was used in Greece, Russia, Tunisia, Sicily and Corsica (by the "Friuli" Division against the German troops).

Technical data 75/18 model 34 howitzers
Piece weight in battery: 780 kg
Vertical shooting sector: -10° + 65°
Horizontal shooting sector: 48°
Grenade weight model 32: 6,35 kg
Initial speed: 425 m/s
Maximum range: 9,5 km

In the Armed Forces of the R.S.I. the 75/18 howitzer was used by the following units:
- "Italy" Bersaglieri Division - 4th Artillery Regiment:
  - II Artillery Group: 3 Batteries - 12 pieces
- "Littorio" Alpine / Grenadiers Division - 2nd Artillery Regiment:
  - The "Gran Sasso" Mountain Group: 1 Battery - 4 pieces
- 1st (51st) Battalion Bersaglieri Coastal Defense (in fixed position on the coast in defense of Genoa): (?) pieces

75/27 gun model 906 and model 911

Krupp's 75mm rapid-firing gun was adopted in 1906 after a long period of experimentation and testing, including with other materials, to replace the old 75A field gun. Production of the piece was interrupted in 1912 following the adoption of the 75/27 Deport but, in 1916, it was resumed by Ansaldo, Armstrong Pozzuoli and the military arsenals following the urgent military needs arising from the war. The 75 Krupp proved to be a good weapon, robust and reliable, with ballistic characteristics comparable to the Austrian pieces. It remained in step with the times until 1917, when the 7.7 cm German FK16 piece with a maximum range of 10.3 km entered the line in the armies of the Central Empire. Destined to be replaced in the Artillery Groups of the Infantry Division by the new materials from 75 nationals, it remained supplied due to the delay in the supply of the new models. In the Royal Army, the 75/27 model 906 was used in horse trailing and mechanical towing groups. In 1912, due to some shortcomings found in the use of the 906 model, poor mobility on varied terrain and a reduced firing range, in addition to the delay in the delivery of the 906 model pieces, it led the Royal Army to reconsider the material supplied to the horse-drawn field artillery. After careful evaluations on Schneider, Krupp and Deport models, the decision was made to adopt the Deport 75 mm deformation cannon with double tail mount, capable of firing at high angles of inclination and direction. Production was entrusted to a consortium of 27 Italian companies chaired by Vickers Terni and the Società Acciaierie di Terni. The 75/27 model 911 gun then joined the 906 model in the Field Artillery Groups, surpassing it in terms of number of pieces in service. After the war, attempts were made to remedy the main shortcomings of the piece: the low range and mobility, in the first case by introducing new projectiles and launch charges, in the second by adapting the cannon to mechanical towing. The 75/27 model 906 gun was used on all fronts except in Russia and East Africa, in Italy also in territorial defense for coastal and anti-landing use and was the most used piece by the Coastal Divisions. The 911 model operated on all fronts except East Africa.

At the outbreak of the conflict, most of the divisional light artillery was still horse-drawn, not even 25% had been adapted to mechanical towing with the adoption of Celerflex semi-pneumatic wheels.

Technical data 75/27 gun model 906
Piece weight in battery: 1015 kg
Vertical shooting sector: -10° + 16°
Horizontal shooting sector: 7°

Grenade weight modello 32: 6,3 kg
Initial speed: 502 m/s
Maximum range: 10,2 km

Technical data 75/27 gun model 911
Piece weight in battery: 1075 kg
Vertical shooting sector: -10° + 65°
Horizontal shooting sector   : 53°
Grenade weight modello 32: 6,3 kg
Initial speed: 502 m/s
Maximum range: 10,2 km

In the Armed Forces of the R.S.I. the 75/27 gun, model 06 or model 11, was used by the following units:
- "Italy" Bersaglieri Division - 4th Artillery Regiment:
    o 2nd Artillery Group: 3 Batteries - 12 pieces[1]
- Infantry Division of the "San Marco" Navy:? pieces in fixed coastal defense positions
- "Littorio" Alpine / Grenadiers Division - 2nd Artillery Regiment:
    o 1st Mountain Group "Gran Sasso": 1 Battery - 4 pieces model 06 in a cave at Chaz Dura (ex G.A.F.)
- "Decima" Navy Infantry Division: "Condottieri" Artillery Regiment:
    o "San Giorgio" Artillery Group: 1 Battery - 4 pieces model 06
- 1st "Benito Mussolini" Bersaglieri Battalion: 2 pieces
- "Leonessa" Armored Group of the G.N.R .: 1 Battery - 4 pieces
- 1st M Battalion "IX Settembre": 2 pieces
- 1st horse-drawn batteries - Autonomous department located in Opicina (TS): 4 pieces
- 1st Coastal Position Artillery Group - 1st Battery: 4 pieces
- 2nd Coastal Position Artillery Group - 7th Battery: 4 pieces
- 12th Artillery Group Coastal Position - 41st Battery: 4 pieces model 06 in a cave position on Monte Croce (ex G.A.F.)
- "Ettore Muti" Mobile Autonomous Legion: 3 Batteries - 12 pieces (also used in anti-aircraft function)

100/17 Howitzer
Skoda production howitzer widely used during the First World War by the Austro-Hungarian Army, it was a modern design gun, well built, solid and robust, highly reliable and with good mobility. It allowed large vertical firing sectors and the power of the grenade was clearly superior to Italian shells. The main shortcomings stemmed from the limited Horizontal shooting sector and the low range. It was built in two models, the country version, model 14, and the specialized one for use in the mountains, model 16, which can be dismantled and towed into three loads. The Royal Army, with the victory over Austria - Hungary, captured and obtained almost two thousand guns of the two models for repairs, thus solving

[1] The 75/27 guns were replaced with the 75/18 howitzers on their return to Italy.

the problem that had tormented him for the duration of the conflict: the lack of a light howitzer to alongside the 75/27 guns in the Field and Mountain Artillery Regiments. In this way, the Skoda 100/17 howitzer became the standard light campaign howitzer of the Royal Army. Many pieces were adapted to mechanical towing, both with the use of the elastic trolley and with the replacement of the wooden spoked wheels with semi-pneumatic rubber wheels. Many howitzers were used for arming fixed positions and in cave fortifications serving in the Guardia Alla Frontiera. It was used on all fronts during World War II, revealing all its limitations deriving from its low range and reduced mobility on various terrain. Despite the poor Initial speed it was also used as an anti-tank weapon.

Technical data 100/17 howitzer
Piece weight in battery: 1415 kg
Vertical shooting sector: -8° + 48°
Horizontal shooting sector: 5°
Grenade weight: 13,3 kg
Initial speed: 407 m/s
Maximum range: 9,2 km

In the Armed Forces of the R.S.I. the 100/17 howitzer was used by the following units:
- Infantry Division of Marina "San Marco" - 3rd Artillery Regiment:
  - 2nd Hippotrained group: 3 Batteries - 12 pieces
  - 3rd Hippotrained group: 3 Batteries - 12 pieces
- "Decima" Navy Infantry Division - "Condottieri" Artillery Regiment:
  - "Colleoni" Artillery Group: 1 Battery - 4 pieces
- Anti Partisans Group – 10th Special Artillery Group - (?) Battery: (?) Pieces
- "Vanni" fighting group (Balkans): 3 pieces
- 2nd Coastal Position Artillery Group - 8th Battery: 4 pieces
- 12th Artillery Group Coastal Position - 37th "Julia" Alpine Battery: 4 model 14 pieces
- 15th Artillery Group Coastal Position - (?) Battery: (?) Pieces
- Coastal Position Artillery Group "Pezzini Group" - FB 16: 4 pieces

100/22 Howitzer

The main deficiency found in the 100/17 howitzer, during the First World War, was the low range. Skoda, immediately after the war, prepared a more powerful version with an elongated barrel which was adopted by numerous European armies. In 1941 the Royal Army came into possession of a few hundred pieces of Czech and Polish origin, sold by the Germans, or captured in Yugoslavia and Greece. The 100/22 howitzer could use the same ammunition as the 100/17 model. It was used in Yugoslavia against the partisans, in Sicily and in the defense of Rome.

Technical data 100/22 howitzer
Grenade weight: 13,3 kg

Initial speed: 415 m/s
Maximum range: 9,6 km

In the Armed Forces of the R.S.I. the 100/22 howitzer was used by the following units:
- "Decima" Navy Infantry Division - "Condottieri" Artillery Regiments:
    o "Colleoni" Artillery Group: 2 Batteries - 8 pieces
- T.M. battery - Autonomous department located in Opicina (TS): 4 pieces

105/28 Gun

The origins of the 105/28 gun date back to 1912, when the Army General Staff decided to introduce a new deformation piece in the heavy field artillery. Two projects were presented and that of Ansaldo, with characteristics similar to the Schneider 105 model 13 model for which it had obtained the construction plans, was chosen. Secretly put into production in September 1914, it arrived at the Departments in July 1915, being produced until 1919 for a total of 1,736 guns and 1,331 barrels. The main shortcomings stemmed from the low power of the grenades and from the excessive wear of the barrel core. After the war, all the pieces were transformed into mechanical towing, both with the use of the elastic trolley and with the replacement of the wooden spoked wheels with tires. It was used in all the operations of the Royal Army after the war, during the World War it was used in all operational theaters.

105/28 gun technical data
Piece weight in battery: 2.470 kg
Vertical shooting sector: -5° +37°
Horizontal shooting sector: 14°
Grenade weight: 16,3 kg
Initial speed: 774 m/s
Maximum range: 13,6 km

Nelle Forze Armate della R.S.I. il cannone da 105/28 venne impiegato dalle seguenti unità:
- "Decima" Navy Infantry Division - "Condottieri" Artillery Regiment:
    o "San Giorgio" Artillery Group: 1 Battery - 4 pieces
- Anti Partisans Group – 10th Special Artillery Group - (?) Batteries: (?) Pieces[2]

105/32 Gun

Cannon produced by Skoda, veteran of the First World War, recovered after the defeat of Austria - Hungary in a few hundred pieces, also during the second conflict remained the piece of heavy field artillery with the greatest range in the Royal Army. He participated in the East African campaign and then was employed in Yugoslavia, Russia, Tunisia and Sicily. The 105/32 gun had a good maximum range, but was much heavier and less maneuverable than the 105/28.

---

[2] According to Giorgio Pisanò (see "History of the Armed Forces of the Italian Social Republic", work cited in the Bibliography) the 2nd Battery of the Group was armed with 4 howitzers of 105/28.

105/32 gun technical data
Piece weight in battery: 3.100 kg
Vertical shooting sector: -10° +30°
Horizontal shooting sector: 6°
Grenade weight: 16,3 kg
Initial speed: 735 m/s
Maximum range: 16,2 km

In the Armed Forces of the R.S.I. the 105/32 cannon was used by the following units:
- "Decima" Navy Infantry Division - "Condottieri" Artillery Regiment:
  - "San Giorgio" Artillery Group: 1 Battery - 4 pieces

149/13 Howitzer

The only howitzer in service in the Heavy Field Artillery Regiments, the 149/13 was a piece of Skoda origin of Austro-Hungarian war prey. After the war, all the pieces were transformed for mechanical towing with a single car, both with the adoption of the elastic trolley and, in the ongoing conflict, using new semi-pneumatic sheet metal wheels. Ballistic capabilities were also improved with the adoption of the new model 32 ammunition. Very robust piece, sufficiently mobile and capable of firing in the second arc of trajectory, it had its limit in the low range and in the scarce firing sector in the direction. It was largely superseded at the start of the conflict by the models serving in the Allied and German armies. It was used in all operational theaters even if from 1940 they were no longer sent to North Africa.

Technical data 149/13 howitzer
Piece weight in battery: 2.765 kg
Vertical shooting sector: -5° +70°
Horizontal shooting sector: 6°
Grenade weight: 42,6 kg
Initial speed: 336 m/s
Maximum range: 8,8 km

In the Armed Forces of the R.S.I. the 149/13 howitzer was used by the following units:
- 14th oastal Position Artillery Group[3] - 32nd and 33rd Battery: 8 pieces
- Coastal Position Artillery Group "Pezzini Group" - FB 15: 4 pieces

149/12 Howitzer

The 149/12 Krupp howitzer remained in service in the Royal Army in the front line departments until the 1920s - 1930s, when it was replaced by 149/13.

Technical data 149/12 Howitzer
Piece weight in battery: 2.344 kg

---
3 In some publications it is referred to as 22nd Group.

Vertical shooting sector: -5° +43°
Horizontal shooting sector: 5°
Maximum range: 6,9 km

In the Armed Forces of the R.S.I. the 149/12 howitzer was used by the following units:
- 10th Artillery Group Coastal Position: (?) Batteries - (?) Pieces

149/19 Howitzer

The 149/19 howitzer was born from a specification issued in 1930 and had a very troubled and complex development, due to the very demanding technical specifications and the difficulties encountered by companies in respecting them, in addition to the continuous changes in the requirements required by the technical bodies of the Regio Army. It had to wait until 1937 to have the final choice of the model presented by OTO, but only in 1941 did mass production begin. Just over a hundred howitzers were built before 8 September, which had its baptism of fire in Sicily in July 1943. A piece with excellent characteristics remained in service in the Italian Army until 1974.

Technical data 149/19 howitzer
Piece weight in battery: 6.260 kg
Vertical shooting sector: -3° +60°
Horizontal shooting sector: 50°
Grenade weight: 42,5 kg
Initial speed: 597 m/s
Maximum range: 14,2 km

In the Armed Forces of the R.S.I. the 149/19 howitzer was used by the following units:
- "Italy" Bersaglieri Division - 4th Artillery Regiment:
    o 3rd Artillery Group: 2 Batteries - 8 pieces
- Alpine / Grenadiers Division "Littorio" – 2nd Artillery Regiment:
    o 4th Campaign Group: 3 Batteries - 12 pieces
- Infantry Division of Marina "San Marco" - 3rd Artillery Regiment:
    o 4th Group T.M.: 3 Batteries - 12 pieces
- 6th Heavy Artillery Group (France): 3 Batteries - 9 pieces
- 1st Coastal Position Artillery Group: 3rd and 4th Battery - 8 pieces
- XIV Artillery Group Coastal Position: 34th Battery: 4 pieces[4]
- Raggruppamento Anti Partigiani 10th Special Artillery Group - (?) Batteries: (?) Pieces[5]

---
[4] In some publications it is referred to as the XXII Group.
[5] According to Giorgio Pisanò (see "Storia delle Forze Armate della Repubblica Sociale Italiana", work cited in the Bibliography) the 4th Battery of the Group was armed with 4 149/19 howitzers.

149/35 Gun

The 149/35 gun originates from studies for a new steel gun around 1890. It was definitively adopted in 1901 and used during the First World War in hundreds of specimens. Appreciated for the power and accuracy of shooting, however, he was constrained by the lack of aiming in the direction, which forced to move the tail of the carriage to correct the aiming, by the slowness of the shot and the rigid carriage, which forced to repeat the aiming every shot. Despite the various attempts made by the arsenals after the war to modify the carriage in a deformation version, the only modification adopted was that of putting into service elastic suspension trains to adapt the gun to mechanical towing. The failure to renovate the artillery park with the adoption of the new 149/40 gun, meant that the Royal Army started the conflict with the anachronistic 149/35 as the only Army artillery. It was used in Libya, France, Greece, Yugoslavia and Sicily. Given the wide availability, many pieces were destined for the arming of fixed positions and forts, as well as used in anti-landing functions on the coasts of Italy, Albania, France, the Aegean, Greece and Dalmatia.

Technical data 149/35 gun
Piece weight in battery: 8.600 kg
Vertical shooting sector: -10° +35°
Grenade weight: 45,9 kg
Initial speed: 628 m/s
Maximum range: 17,5 km

In the Armed Forces of the R.S.I. the 149/35 gun was used by the following units:
- "Littorio" Alpine / Grenadiers Division - 2nd Artillery Regiment:
  o 1st "Gran Sasso" Mountain Group: 2 pieces belonging to the fortifications of the Vallo del Littorio (ex G.A.F.)
- 13th Artillery Group Coastal Position: 38th, 39th and 40th Battery - 12 pieces
- 17th Artillery Group Coastal Position: (?) Batteries: (?) Pieces

210/8 Mortar

Piece of Italian conception dating back to 1891, it was used as siege artillery throughout the First World War. During the conflict, the mortar was installed on De Angelis platform or De Stefanis model carriages, much cheaper than the original Schneider carriage. In 1936 the alienation of all 210/8 materials was decided. In 1939, of the 500 existing pieces, only 180 were still available for the constitution of 45 Batteries to be used as a static reinforcement to the coverage sectors of the GAF or ports. It was used against France and during the attack on Yugoslavia.

Technical data 210/8 mortar (De Stefano)
Piece weight in battery: 10.310 kg
Vertical shooting sector: -15° +70°
Horizontal shooting sector: 360°
Grenade weight: 101 kg
Initial speed: 345 m/s
Maximum range: 8,4 km

In the Armed Forces of the R.S.I. the 210/8 mortar was used by the following units:
- "Littorio" Alpini / Grenadiers Division – 2nd Artillery Regiment:
  - 2nd Mountain Group "Romagna": 1 piece

▲ In this image, unfortunately of poor quality, because it comes from the periodical published by the "Ettore Muti" Mobile Autonomous Legion of Milan portrays an ancient 65/17 cannon supplied in the department (Sandri Archive).

▼ Howitzers 75/13 of the "Vicenza" Artillery Group on the western Alps front ("Monterosa" Archive).

▲ Training in Germany of the "Vicenza" Artillery Group of the "Monterosa" Division ("Monterosa" Archive).

▼ A 75/13 howitzer of the "Vicenza" Artiglieri Group in action on the front of the Western Alps ("Monterosa" Archive).

▲ Group photo of the servants of a 75/13 howitzer of the "Aosta" Artillery Group of the "Monterosa" Division in position in Avegno (GE) (Cucut Collection).

▼ The 4th piece of the "Bergamo" Artillery Group of the "Monterosa" Division camouflaged on the front of the Gothic Line in Garfagnana ("Monterosa" Archive).

▲ One of the 75/13 howitzers in service at the "Ettore Muti" Mobile Autonomous Legion of Milan. The legionaries wear a peculiar black uniform, distributed only to members of the "Mezzi Pesanti" Company (Sandri Archive).

▼ 75/13 Howitzer of the "Bergamo" Artillery Group of the "Monterosa" Division ("Monterosa" Archive).

▲ The fighting conditions on the Gothic Line in Garfagnana were very harsh, as can be seen in this image showing a 75/13 howitzer of the "Bergamo" Artillery Group of the "Monterosa", ready to open fire ("Monterosa" Archive).

▼ On the western front, the "Gran Sasso" Artillery Group of the 2nd Artillery Regiment of the "Littorio" Division set up its 75/13 howitzers (Arena Archive).

▲ Another image of a 75/13 howitzer of the "Gran Sasso" Artillery Group, deployed at the Piccolo San Bernardo (Quaquaro Archive).

▼ Italian gunners of one of the Divisions trained in Germany receive instruction in the use of the 75/13 howitzer (Arena Archive).

▲ A 75/13 howitzer of the "San Giorgio" Artillery Group of the "Condottieri" Regiment of the "Decima" Division fires during the battle of Tarnova in January 1945: the piece is photographed at the moment of maximum recoil (Panzarasa Archive).

▼ Section of howitzers from 75/13 "San Giorgio" Artillery Group of the "Condottieri" Regiment during the battle of Tarnova (Panzarasa Archive).

▲ Legionaries of the Waffen-Artillerie-Abteilung of the Italian SS show a 75/13 howitzer to the young students of the Republican National Guard School of Rivoli (TO). The piece was transported aboard a FIAT 626 truck, as often happened (Arena Archive).

▼ An Italian SS 75 mountain howitzer ready to fire (Arena Archive).

▲ 75/27 model 911 gun in service in the 7th Battery of the II Artillery Group Coastal Position on the Ligurian coast (Scarone Archive).

▼ 75/27 gun mod. 906 in service in the "Ettore Muti" Mobile Autonomous Legion (Sandri Archive).

▲ A 100/17 howitzer in service in the 37th "Julia" Battery, which was located on Monte Lesco, near Fiume (Crivellari Archive).

▼ Shooting with the 100/17 howitzer in the 37th "Julia" Battery (Crivellari Archive).

▲ This unit of the Republican National Guard, probably attached to the Pz.Abt.208, was equipped with a 100/17 howitzer, with a showy three-color camouflage (Tallillo Archive).

▼ An 100/17 howitzer of the X MAS towed by a truck of the "Fulmine" Battalion (Arena Archive).

▲ Borghese Commander, visiting the "Colleoni" Artillery Group of the "Condottieri" Regiment on the Senio front, observes one of the 100/17 pieces (Panzarasa Archive).

▼ On the Senio front, a 100/17 howitzer of the "Colleoni" Group is prepared for fire by the servants, wearing the typical camouflage garments distributed to the marines of the "Decima" (Panzarasa Archive).

▲ A 100/17 howitzer in service in the 2nd Artillery Group of the 3rd Artillery Regiment of the "San Marco" Division in the Savona area (Baldrati Archive).

▼ Position of the X Mas with a 105/28 gun of the 1st Speranza Battery of the "San Giorgio on the front of Neptune" Artillery Group (Panzarasa Archive).

▲ 105/32 cannon of the 2nd Battery of the "San Giorgio" Artillery Group in Nettuno (Panzarasa Archive).

▼ Soldiers of the 4th Artillery Group 2nd Regiment of the "Littorio" Division are trained in the use of the howitzer from 149/19 in Germany (Viziano Archive).

▲ Howitzer from 149/19 of the IV Artillery Group 2nd Regiment of the "Littorio" Division ready to fire on the western Alps front (Viziano Archive).

▼ 149/19 Howitzer of the 3rd Artillery Group, 4th Regiment of the "Italy" Division, placed in battery in a highly camouflaged position in the rear of the Gothic Line (Viziano Archive).

▲ 7.5 cm cannon. the IG 18 in service in the "Folgore" Parachute Regiment (Arena Archive).

▼ The paratroopers of the "Folgore" Regiment observe this 7.5 cm gun. the IG 18, which was supplied to the department (Arena Archive).

▲ Bersaglieri of the "Italy" Division in training in Germany with the 7.5 cm gun. the IG 18 (Viziano Archive).

▼ Bersaglieri of the "Italy" Division set up a 7.5 cm gun. the IG 18 on the Gothic Line (Viziano Archive).

▲ These Bersaglieri of the "Italia" Division on the Gothic line have camouflaged themselves and their 7.5 cm gun. the IG 18 with white sheets and sheets, to blend into the abundantly fallen snow (Viziano Archive).

▼ The "Cadelo" Exploring Group of the "Monterosa" Division was also equipped with a 7.5 cm cannon. Le IG 18: here a piece photographed on the Gothic Line ("Monterosa" Archive).

▲ A 7.5 cm gun. the. IG 18 is transported by Arditi of the III Exploring Group of the "San Marco" Division (Baldrati Archive).

▼ Arditi of the III Exploring Group of the "San Marco" Division ready to fire with a 7.5 cm cannon. the. IG 18 on the Ligurian coast (Baldrati Archive).

▲ 7.5 cm GebG 36 mountain gun used by the 5th Battery of the "Romagna" Mountain Group II of the "Littorio" Division in Larche (Cucut Archive).

▼ 7.5 cm GebG 36 mountain cannon in position in the Western Alps ("Monterosa" Archive).

▲ Alpini of the 5th Battery of the II Romagna Mountain Group of the "Littorio" Division at high altitude in Larche with a 7.5 cm GebG 36 mountain piece (Acta Archive).

▼ The Alpini of the "Mantova" Artillery Group were trained in the use of the 10.5 cm howitzer. The FH 18 during their stay in the Munsingen camp in Germany ("Monterosa" Archive).

▲ Alpine artillerymen of the 4th Battery of the "Mantova" Artillery Group of the "Monterosa" Division, deployed in the Aosta Valley, around a 10.5 cm howitzer LE FH 18 ("Monterosa" Archive).

▼ Minions of a 10.5 cm howitzer LE FH 18 of the "Mantova" Artillery Group of the "Monterosa" prepare the piece for fire in Garfagnana ("Monterosa" Archive).

▲ Artillerymen of the "Mantova" Artillery Group of the "Monterosa" Division marching towards the front with a 10.5 cm howitzer, moved by animal tow ("Monterosa" Archive).

▼ 10.5 cm howitzer LE FH 18 of the "Mantova" Artillery Group of the "Monterosa" Division ready to fire in Garfagnana ("Monterosa" Archive).

▲ SIG-33 15 cm howitzer, exhibited at the Belgrade Museum, supplied to the "Italy" Bersaglieri Division during training in Germany.

▲ 76.2 M1939 gun, preserved in the Moscow Museum, supplied to the "Vanni" Group.

▲ Artillerymen of the Coastal Position Artillery Group put a 105/27 French gun into battery, in service at the FB 14 battery (Cucut Archive).

▼ French 105/27 cannon of the FB 14 Battery of the P.C. Artillery Group "Pezzini" (Cucut Archive).

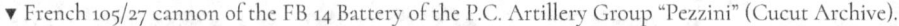

FOREIGN ARTILLERY

7,5 cm. le IG 18 (leichte Infanterie Geschutz) Gun
German piece developed by Rheinmetall in 1927, it went into distribution in the early thirties, being assigned to the Infantry Cannon Companies, and subsequently to the Heavy Weapons Companies of the Panzergranadier Regiments and to the Motorized Infantry. In 1937 it was mounted on a lightened carriage and distributed to the mountain troops as a 75 mm "leichte Gebirges" IG 18.

In the Armed Forces of the R.S.I. the 75/10 IG 18 gun was used by the following units:
- "Italy" Bersaglieri Division – 4th Exploring Group: 10 pieces expected, in January 1945 there were 4 in service
- Infantry Division of Marina "San Marco" – 3rd Exploring Group: 2 pieces[6]
- "Monterosa" Alpine Division – 1st "Cadelo" Exploring Group: 13 pieces
- "Folgore" Parachute Regiments: there are photographs that testify to the presence of the piece in service, but there is no news regarding its actual use on the Western Alps Front.
- 2nd (20th) Voluntary Bersaglieri Coastal Defense Battalions: also in this case there are photographs that testify to the presence of the piece in service, but there is no information regarding its actual use.

7,5 cm GebG 36 Mountain gun
The 7.5 cm Gebirgsgeschütz 36, abbreviated to 7.5 cm GebG 36, was a German mountain gun. It was the standard light gun of the mountain divisions of both the Heer and Waffen SS during World War II, introduced in 1938 to replace the antiquated models.

In the Armed Forces of the R.S.I. the 75/21 gun was used by the following units:
- "Littorio" Alpine / Grenadiers Division - 2nd Artillery Regiment:
    o 2nd Mountain Group "Romagna": 5th Battery - 4 pieces

10,5 cm. le FH 18 (leichte Feld Haubitze) Howitzer
Regulatory campaign howitzer in service in the German artillery, it was introduced in 1935. Excellent piece with characteristics equivalent to the American 105 and the British 88, easy to handle, easy to use and firm when firing. In order to improve its performance, the FH 18M version (M = Mundungbremse) was produced, equipped with a muzzle brake and a recoil system adjusted to allow the use of a more powerful charge and a long-range grenade.

Technical data 105 FH18 Howitzer
Piece weight in battery: 2.000 kg
Vertical shooting sector: -5° +42°
Horizontal shooting sector: 56°

---
6 Some documents show a total of 10 pieces in service in the Division.

Grenade weight: 14,8 kg
Initial speed: 470/540 m/s
Maximum range: 12,3 km

In the Armed Forces of the R.S.I. of the 10.5 cm howitzer Le FH18 was used by the following units:
- "Monterosa" Alpine Division - 1st Artillery Regiment:
   o 4th "Mantova" horse trainee group: 3 Batteries - 12 pieces

15 cm sIG-33 (15 cm schweres Infanterie Geschütz 1933) Howitzer

Accompanying piece for the infantry, requested by the German General Staff in the 1920s, developed by Rheinmetall starting in 1927 and accepted by the army in 1933. Initially produced only by Rheinmetall, it was then also built by AEG - Fabrik and later by Böhmische Waffenfabrik. In total 4,600 pieces were built. It was normally pulled by horses, only at low speed it could be pulled by vehicles. It was modernized with the replacement of the original wheels with others equipped with tires. Already during the Polish campaign, the poor mobility of the howitzer emerged, which prevented support for the infantry. Many howitzers were then destined for transformation into self-propelled ones. He remained in service until the end of the conflict.

Technical data 150 sIG 33 Howitzer
Piece weight in battery: kg 1.750
Vertical shooting sector: +73°
Horizontal shooting sector: 11,5°
Grenade weight: 38 kg HE
Initial speed: 240 m/s
Maximum range: 4,7 km

In the Armed Forces of the R.S.I. the 150 SIG 33 howitzer was used by the following units:
- "Italy" Bersaglieri Division: a Batteries with 4 pieces planned, only one piece in service for training in Germany. There are no SIG 33 howitzers in service in Italy.

76,2 M1939 Gun

Soviet campaign cannon, adopted by the Red Army in 1939, was produced by Plant N ° 92 in Grabin and, during the war, by the Barrikadi factory in Stalingrad in thousands of pieces until the end of 1943, when it was replaced by the ZiS-3 . Also referred to as the F-22 USV, it was used in the batteries of light artillery regiments. Also excellent in counter-tank function, hundreds of pieces were captured by the Germans, who reused them by converting many of them into anti-tank guns, with the denomination 7.62 PaK 39 (r).

Technical data 76,2 gun
Piece weight in battery: 1.470 kg
Vertical shooting sector: -6° + 45°

Horizontal shooting sector: 60°
Grenade weight: da 4.2 a 7,1 kg according to the bullets used
Initial speed: da 624 a 1.025 m/s according to the bullets used
Maximum range: da 4 a 13.29 km according to the bullets used

In the Armed Forces of the R.S.I. the 76.2 gun was used by the following units:
- "Vanni" fighting group (Balkans): 8 pieces

105/27 Gun

Heavy field material of French war prey, built by Schneider as 105 L model 13, sold by the Germans or obtained through the Italian Armistice Commission with France (CIAF). It was used as an anti-landing and coastal defense function. It could use the same ammunition as the Italian 105/28.

Technical data 105/27 gun
Piece weight in battery: 2.300 kg
Vertical shooting sector: -5° + 37°
Horizontal shooting sector: 6°
Grenade weight: 5,7 kg
Initial speed: 550 m/s
Maximum range: 12 km

In the Armed Forces of the R.S.I. the 105/27 gun was used by the following units:
- Coastal Position Artillery Group "Pezzini Group" - FB 14: 4 pieces

ANTI-TANK ARTILLERY

In this section all the guns, Italian or foreign, specifically built with the anti-tank fighting function have been included. In the departments of the R.S.I. they were almost constantly used, rather than in the main task of fighting the tank, as a support to the infantry. This role was particularly suitable for small caliber guns, now unusable against modern Allied tanks.

ITALIAN ARTILLERY

47/32 gun
Ordinary repeating weapon with Böhler patent, but Italian construction Breda, was adopted in 1935 to compensate for the lack of an anti-tank weapon and to replace the old 65/17 pieces to accompany the infantry. Its anti-tank characteristics, excellent upon entry into service, became modest as early as 1940 and insufficient with the appearance of the new medium and heavy tanks in 1942. It was produced in large quantities in two models, the model 35, resembling and self-transportable, and the model 39, self-towable. It was the standard cannon of the anti-tank companies and the only cannon supplied to paratroop troops. It was used on all fronts, in some cases even aboard vans or other vehicles. It was the basic weapon of the Italian medium tanks. Particularly felt the lack of a protection shield and a small car for towing the piece, of the type used in other Armies, such as the Dutch one.

Technical data 47/32 model 35 gun
Piece weight in battery: 277 kg
Vertical shooting sector: -10° +56°
Horizontal shooting sector: 60°
Grenade weight: 1,4 kg
Initial speed: 630 m/s
Maximum range: 7 km (700 m in anti-tank use)

In the Armed Forces of the R.S.I. the 47/32 cannon was used by the following units:
- 29th Waffen-Grenadier Division der SS - Italienische n.1: 8 pieces
- "Decima" Navy Infantry Division:
    - "Barbarigo" Battalion: 2 pieces
    - "Lupo" Battalion: 2 pieces
    - "Valanga" Battalion: 2 pieces model 39
- "Ettore Muti" Mobile Autonomous Legion: 2 pieces
- Black Brigade "Ather Capelli": 2 pieces
- "Tagliamento" Alpine Regiments: 15 pieces (one for each company plus six at the "Montenero" Company)
- 1st (51st) Coastal Defense Bersaglieri Battalion: (?) Pieces
- 2nd (20th) Coastal Defense Bersaglieri Battalion: 4 pieces (one per company)
- 5th Coastal Defense Battalion: 2 pieces
- Grouping of "Hunters of the Apennines": (?) Pieces
- 1st Battalion "Grenadiers of Sardinia": (?) Pieces
- Raggruppamento Anti Partigiani: (?) Pieces

FOREIGN ARTILLERY

20 mm S anti-tank rifle
Improved version of the Solothurn 20 mm universal rifle made by the Swiss company Waffenfabrik in 1933 / '35, it was introduced into the Royal Army in 1940, with the first specimens delivered to the 10th Army in Libya. It used the same 20 gauge cartridge of the Italian Breda and Scotti - Isotta Fraschini - OM and of the German Rheinmetall. It could be used both on the special transport trolley and on a biped. During the conflict it was also placed on board vehicles, desert vans, and L3 wagons. It was mainly used in Northern Africa.

Technical data 20 mm S anti-tank riflemodel 39
Weapon weight: 54,7 kg
Total weight with trolley: 127 kg
Vertical shooting sector: -0° +10°
Horizontal shooting sector: 50°
Grenade weight: 135 gr
Initial speed: 832 m/s
Maximum range: 1.500 m

In the Armed Forces of the R.S.I. the 20 mm counter-tank rifle was used by the following units:
- 15th "Benito Mussolini" Coastal Defense Battalion: 1 or 2 pieces
- Battalion "Lightning" Infantry Division of the Navy "Decima": 2 pieces
- Mobile Autonomous Legion "Ettore Muti": at least 3 pieces

Hotchkiss da 25/72 Gun model 34 and model 37
Produced by the French Hotchkiss in two versions, model 34 and 37, it became one of the regulative artillery materials of the Royal Army after the brief conflict with France in 1940, following which it obtained 43 complexes under the armistice clauses and another 250 from Germany . The muzzle was mounted on a 2-tailed carriage, equipped with pneumatic wheels and a shield with an edged upper edge to confuse remote identification. It was endowed with good piercing power, despite its small caliber, thanks to the high initial speed and the tungsten core grenade foil. The large horizontal shooting sector and the reduced vertical shape are noteworthy. Weaknesses, the considerable weight and the lack of an armor-piercing bullet. On 25/72 the motorized and infantry divisions were strengthened in North Africa, where it was also used in Tunisia. Some pieces were used in coastal defense and anti-landing functions.

Technical data 25/72 gun
Piece weight in battery: 480 kg
Horizontal shooting sector: 60°
Initial speed: 950 m/s

In the Armed Forces of the R.S.I. the 25/72 gun was used by the following units:
- 5th Coastal Defense Battalion: 2 pieces
- 15th "Benito Mussolini" Coastal Defense Battalion: 6 pieces
- 16th Coastal Defense Battalion: 1 piece

3,7 cm. PaK – 35/36 Gun

Built on a Rheinmetall-Borsig project in the 1930s, it was used by Italian troops already during the Spanish War, where 40 cannons were used to reinforce the anti-tank defenses of the Voluntary Troops Corps. During the Abyssinian campaign, the 30 specimens supplied to the Ethiopians were captured intact and subsequently used by the Royal Army against the British in 1940 - '41. During the war the Germans ceded various pieces to the Royal Army which used them in Libya starting from 1941. The 37/45 in the early 1940s was already an inadequate piece against modern medium and heavy tanks, however it still retained a decent validity in infantry support. Excellent weapon, precise, easy to handle, small in shape, well protected against small arms fire, with the pointer that could maneuver the swing, tilt and firing handwheels at the same time. It was used to arm self-propelled vehicles and tanks. Some specimens captured in Russia were reused by the CSIR and ARMIR Departments. Over 15,000 copies were produced.

Technical data 37/45 gun
Piece weight in battery: 444 kg
Vertical shooting sector: -8° +25°
Horizontal shooting sector: 59°
Grenade weight: 700 gr
Initial speed: 745 m/s
Maximum range: 800 m

In the Armed Forces of the R.S.I. the 37/45 gun was used by the following units:
- 1st Legion M assault "Tagliamento" G.N.R.: 3 pieces

45 mm M1937 (53-k) Gun

Soviet-made anti-tank gun, captured in large quantities during the initial offensive, was the evolution of the 37 mm model 30. Outdated as an anti-tank gun, it was used as a support gun.

Technical data 45 mm M1937 gun
Piece weight in battery: 560 kg
Vertical shooting sector: -8° + 25°
Horizontal shooting sector: 60°
Initial speed: 760 m/s

In the Armed Forces of the R.S.I. the 45 model 37 gun was used by the following units:
- 16th Coastal Defense Battalion: 1 piece

7,5 cm. PaK 40 Gin

Designed by Rheinmetall, it was basically the enlarged version of the 5 cm PaK-38. Equipped with excellent ballistic performance and with small dimensions, it was criticized for its excessive weight that made it unwieldy and mobile on varied terrain. Built in thousands of units, the PaK 40 was the main anti-tank weapon of the German army in the last three years of the war and was also used to arm self-propelled vehicles, tank destroyers, tanks and armed trains. In 1945, with increasingly improved ammunition, it was able to pierce the frontal armor of all the main Russian and allied tanks. In June 1943 the Royal Army decided to adopt it and reproduce it under license, with an order for 1,000 copies. By the date of the armistice, only a few dozen specimens had been delivered, of which 42 used for coastal defense tasks in Greece and the Aegean.

Technical data 75/43 model 40 gun
Piece weight in battery: 1.425 kg
Vertical shooting sector: -5° +22°
Horizontal shooting sector: 65°
Grenade weight: 3,2 kg
Initial speed: 933 m/s

In the Armed Forces of the R.S.I. the 75/43 gun was used by the following units:
- "Italy" Bersaglieri Division: (?) 17 pieces provided in the armament tables (probably a Batterie with 4 pieces)
- "Littorio" Alpini / Grenadiers Division: 20 pieces (?) (there is the certainty of at least 1 Batteries with 4 pieces)
- Marines Division "San Marco": 22 pieces (?) (Probably only provided in the tables)
- "Monterosa" Alpine Division: 20 pieces (some pieces were later replaced with Panzerschrecks)
- 29th Waffen-Grenadier Division der SS - Italienische n.1: (?) Pieces

▲ 47/32 cannon ready to fire from the "Valanga" Battalion of the "Decima" Navy Infantry Division. The soldiers wear the typical camouflage suit of the marines and have depicted, on the left side of the helmet, the tricolor (Roberti Archive).

▼ Marò of the "Valanga" Battalion in training with a 47/32 anti-tank gun in the Vittorio Veneto area, winter 1944 (Roberti Archive).

▲ Another image of the exercise depicted in the previous photograph: the soldiers of the "Valanga" have placed the 47/32 gun in position, which is now ready to fire (Roberti Archive).

▼A 47/32 gun emplacement of the "Tagliamento" Alpine Regiment in Tolmino (Archive of the "Tagliamento" Alpine Regiment).

▲ Bersaglieri of the "Isonzo" Battalion of the "Tagliamento" Alpine Regiment in Canale with a 47/32 gun (Archive of the "Tagliamento" Alpine Regiment).

▼ The two 47/32 anti-tank guns of the 1st Black Brigade "Ather Capelli" of Turin portrayed together with a 20 mm machine gun and a Autocarretta in a rare photograph dating back to the winter of 1944 - '45, published in the magazine of the time "Time Signal" (Monti - Satiz).

▲ Legionaries with 47/32 cannon of the 29th Waffen-Grenadier Division der SS - Italienische n.1 (Arena Archive).

▼ Evocative image of a counter-tank piece of the Italian SS, ready to fire (Pisanò Archive).

▲ Bersaglieri of the "Mussolini" Battalion with a 20 mm Solothurn anti-tank rifle (Cucut Archive).

▼ Ceremony for the delivery of the pennant to the "Fulmine" Battalion of the "Decima" Division in Piazza Castello in Turin in October 1944. In the foreground, the 20 mm Solothurn anti-tank rifles supplied to the department can be seen (Panzarasa Archive).

▲ Three Solothurn rifles were also in service at the "Ettore Muti" Legion in Milan, in this image ready to be towed during a magazine (Crippa Archive).

▼ A German soldier trains an Italian fellow soldier to shoot with the PaK 37 anti-tank gun (Arena Archive).

▲ A 37 mm anti-tank gun is quickly brought to position by legionaries of the "Tagliamento" during a round-up operation in Central Italy in the summer of 1944. The piece, ready to fire, was camouflaged with branches (Pisanò Archive).

▼ The Accompanying Arms Company of the "Tagliamento" deployed in full: in addition to the three PAK 37 cannons, the department also had 7 81 mm mortars (Pisanò Archive).

▲ Shooting tests with anti-tank guns of the "Tagliamento" Legion in the summer of 1944: the soldiers wear the summer uniform of the G.N.R., consisting of a Saharan jacket and khaki-colored shorts (Pisanò Archive).

▼ Russian 45 mm gun M1937 (53-k) Russian in service at the Drenova stronghold of the 16th Coastal Defense Battalion (Cucut Archive).

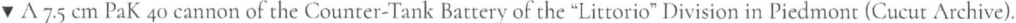

▲ Marò of the "San Marco" Division in training in Germany with 7.5 cm guns. PaK 40 (Monterosa Archive).

▼ A 7.5 cm PaK 40 cannon of the Counter-Tank Battery of the "Littorio" Division in Piedmont (Cucut Archive).

▲ 7.5 cm PaK 40 cannons of the units of the Italian Social Republic captured by the partisans in Cuorgnè (TO) (Istoreto Archive).

▼ 7.5 cm PaK 40 cannons of the Exploring Group of the "Monterosa" Division on the railway platforms during the return to Italy from Germany ("Monterosa" Archive).

▲ Artillerymen from a large unit of the Republican National Army prepare a PaK 40 anti-tank gun for fire (Arena Archive).

▼ Soldiers of the 1.Batterie der Waffen-Panzerjaeger-Abteilung der SS of the 29th Italian SS Legion show the students of the G.N.R. of Rivoli a Pak 40 anti-tank gun (Arena Archive).

▲ The Waffen-Panzerjaeger-Abteilung der SS used TL37 tractors to tow its PaK 40 anti-tank parts (Arena Archive).

ANTI-AIRCRAFT ARTILLERY

In this section all the Italian or foreign anti-aircraft guns and machine guns have been included. In the R.S.I. the anti-aircraft defense was delegated to the A.N.R., which included the Anti-aircraft Artillery (Ar.Co.). The bow. it was structured on 6 Antiaircraft Groups united in two Regiments, and each Group was normally made up of Command Batteries and from 4 to 8 AA Batteries. The anti-aircraft guns were assisted by the "Gamma" and B.G.S. firing centers, enslaved by the "Wurzburg" funkmess. The bow. operated in close contact with Flak Italien. It can be safely argued that only during the R.S.I. the anti-aircraft defense of the Italian territory reached a qualitative-quantitative level never reached in previous years. In the low-altitude defense against Allied fighter-bombers, both military and civilian targets, hundreds of machine gunners were used. To the Departments of the Ar.Co. 128 killings are attributed. The 20mm machine guns were used both in the natural original anti-aircraft function, and, above all in many small undivided wards, as an accompanying weapon and support to the infantry during counter-guerrilla actions.

ITALIAN ARTILLERY

Breda machine gun 20/65 model 35
In 1935 the 20 mm gun-gun made by Breda as early as 1932 was adopted for anti-aircraft defense at low altitude and for counter-tank shooting. It was built in two models, the 35 model on a rotating platform carriage, with tails, convertible for towing on wheeled carriage and model 39 for fixed position. The last examples produced had small diameter wheels in elektron. Almost all the complexes produced during the war and those mounted on the trucks had the simplified aiming device. Built in large quantities, it was also installed on light tanks, armored cars and vans. Effective weapon for low-altitude shooting against aircraft, it had similar performances to the best foreign achievements, however, towards the middle of the conflict it was considered outdated. It was used on all fronts.

Technical data gun 20/65 model 35
Piece weight in battery: 330 kg
Vertical shooting sector: -10° +80°
Horizontal shooting sector: 360°
Grenade weight: 135 gr
Initial speed: 840 m/s
Maximum range: 5,5 km – 2,7 km (a.a).

In the Armed Forces of the R.S.I. the 20/65 machine gun was used by the following units:
- Ar.Co .: (?) Batteries (?) Pieces
- "Italia" Bersaglieri Division: (?) Pieces

- Alpini / Grenadiers Division "Littorio": (?) Pieces
- Naval Infantry Division "San Marco": (?) Pieces
- "Monterosa" Alpine Division: 15 pieces
- "Decima" Naval Infantry Division:
    - "Sagittario" Battalion: 1 piece
    - "Lupo" Battalion: 4 pieces
    - "Alberto Da Giussano" Artillery Group: 4 pieces
    - Anti-aircraft Group "Q": (?) pieces
- 29th Waffen-Grenadier Division der SS - Italienische n.1: 2 pieces (check, probably the number was higher)
- "Ettore Muti" Mobile Autonomous Legion: 9 pieces
- Black Brigade "Ather Capelli": 1 piece
- "Leoncello" Armored Squadron Group: 4 pieces
- 1st (51st) Coastal Defense Bersaglieri Battalions: (?) Pieces
- 4th (18th) Coastal Defense Bersaglieri Battalions: (?) Pieces
- 6th Coastal Defense Battalions: (?) Pieces (at least 2)
- 16th Coastal Defense Battalions: 1 piece
- 15th "Benito Mussolini" Coastal Defense Battalions: 6 pieces
- Raggruppamento "Cacciatori degli Appennini": (?) Pieces
- Territorial Defense Militia (G.N.R.): (?) Pieces
- 12th Artillery Group Coastal Position: 1 piece

Scotti-Isotta Fraschini - O.M. 20/70 Machine gun

The prototype dates back to 1932 and the first model was built by Isotta Fraschini, in 1938 it was improved, in 1939 it was defined, but only in 1941 was it adopted by the Royal Army as model 41, while in the Regia Aeronautica and in the Regia Marina it was already in service. model 39 on stanchion carriage for use on land and on board. The ballistic characteristics and ammunition did not differ from those of the 35 model. Two position models were made and used, one of which on a simplified carriage.

Technical data 20/70 machine gun
Piece weight in battery: 386 kg
Vertical shooting sector: -10° +85°
Grenade weight: 135 gr
Initial speed: 830 m/s

In the Armed Forces of the R.S.I. the 20/70 machine gun was used by the following units:
- Ar.Co .: (?) Batteries (?) Pieces
- "Ettore Muti" Mobile Autonomous Legion: (?) Pieces on Alfa Romeo 800 truck, at least 2 pieces mounted on armored carts, (?) Pieces towed by light trucks.

Breda 37/54 Machine gun

Adopted by the Royal Navy in 1932 on a twin carriage, it was selected in 1939 by the Royal Army in a pedestal installation for single position weapon. At the request of the Royal Army, in 1941, the Breda mounted the weapon on a model 41 cross carriage for the low-medium altitude protection of the field units, which was however discarded in favor of the 40/56 Bofors. It was the main medium-range anti-aircraft weapon supplied to the Royal Army, the Royal Navy and the Militia. It was used in North and East Africa, the Aegean, the Balkans and the Peninsula. A total of 18 batteries participated in the defense of Sicily.

Technical data 37/54 machine gun
Piece weight in battery: 2.975 kg
Vertical shooting sector: -0° +90°
Horizontal shooting sector: 360°
Grenade weight: 828 gr
Initial speed: 800 m/s
Maximum range: 6,8 km – 4 km a.a.

In the Armed Forces of the R.S.I. the 37/54 machine gun was used by the following units:
- "Decima" Navy Infantry Division:
    o "Condottieri" Artillery Regiment - "Colleoni" Artillery Group: 1 piece
    o Anti-aircraft group "Q": (?) pieces
- Ar.Co .: (?) Batteries (?) Pieces

75/46 Gun

Progettato dall'Ansaldo venne realizzato in 10 esemplari di preserie nel 1932 ed adottato, nel 1933, dopo i soddisfacenti esiti delle prove a fuoco. Nel 1939 erano disponibili 92 esemplari. Il 75/46 era una buona arma contraerei: forte Initial speed, elevata celerità di tiro, ampi settori di tiro verticale ed orizzontale, congegni di puntamento idonei al tiro diretto e indiretto. Montato su affusto a crociera munito di carrello elastico a ruote ed avantreno per il traino meccanico, venne prodotto in tre versioni: modello 34 campale, modello 34 M campale con traino meccanico semplificato e possibilità di impiego in associazione a centrale di tiro tipo Gamma, modello40 DICAT da posizione. Nell'impiego come pezzo antiaereo da posizione fu presto superato, causa alcuni inconvenienti tecnici che diminuirono sensibilmente l'ordinata massima, non consentendo di raggiungere le quote alle quali operavano i bombardieri Alleati. Venne utilizzato anche come arma controcarro, dove ottenne discreti successi. Venne impiegato durante la guerra di Spagna, dove ebbe il battesimo del fuoco, quindi in Africa orientale e settentrionale, Grecia, Russia e Sicilia. Nel 1941 la versione autocampale assunse la denominazione di cannone contraerei e controcarro da 75/46. Dopo l'8 settembre armò pochi semoventi cacciacarri su scafo del carro M impiegati dai tedeschi.

Technical data 75/46 gun
Piece weight in battery: 3.330 kg
Vertical shooting sector: -0° +90°
Horizontal shooting sector: 360°
Grenade weight: 6,5 kg
Initial speed: 750 m/s
Maximum range: 13 km – 8,5 km a.a.

In the Armed Forces of the R.S.I. the 75/46 cannon was used by the following units:
- Ar.Co .:
    - 4th Group "Cavalli": 2 Batteries - 8 pieces
    - 6th Group "Paganuzzi": 2 Batteries - 8 pieces

76/40 Gun

Piece designed by the English Armstrong, it was adopted by the Royal Navy in 1897 and reproduced under license in Italy by Armstrong Pozzuoli and by the Naval Arsenals, as well as by Vickers Terni during the First World War. In 1935 240 guns were assigned to the territorial anti-aircraft defense, taking them from the Regia Marina. These pieces were modified by mounting them on a new pedestal carriage of new design, designed by the Arsenale of Venice and produced by Ansaldo and Breda. These pieces took the name of 76/40 model 35 and were used by MACA and by the anti-aircraft groups of the Royal Army. In the first years of the war it was already inadequate, due to the poor orderliness attainable.

Technical data 76/40 gun
Horizontal shooting sector: 360°
Grenade weight: 6 kg
Initial speed: 690 m/s
Maximum range: 12,7 km – 6 km c.a.

In the Armed Forces of the R.S.I. the 76/40 gun was used by the following units:
- Ar.Co .: (?) Batteries (?) Pieces
- 9th Artillery Group Coastal Position: 2 Batteries - 8 pieces
- 11th Artillery Group Coastal Position: (?) Batteries - (?) Pieces

90/53 Gun

In 1938 the Royal Army decided to adopt a more powerful anti-aircraft gun than the 75/46, capable of hitting bombers at altitudes of over 10 km. A 90 mm Ansaldo project being studied on behalf of the Regia Marina was considered. In April 1939, the Genoese company was given the task of preparing a derivative version for land use. In January 1940 the first position complex was completed. The tests took place in Nettunia in April 1940 and, given the positive outcome, it was decided to proceed with series production. An attempt was made to unify the versions for the Royal Navy and the Royal Army but, failing to find an agreement, they proceeded to build the 90/53 for the Royal Army and the 90/50 for the Royal Navy. During the conflict, however, both the Navy and MILMART used numerous 90/53, while the Royal Army evaluated the opportunity to use the 90/50 for the defense of Rome. In addition to Ansaldo, OTO, Officine Reggiane, Comerio, Officine di Gorizia, CRDA, Galileo, San Giorgio were involved in the production, as regards the construction of the trolleys and aiming tools. More complex speech for the trolleys intended for field complexes. Following lengthy tests on three different prototypes, the Ansaldo platform wagon was chosen and the order was passed to Motomeccanica, which, however, received the construction license only in June 1941. The first platforms for 90/53 model 41 C guns were delivered only at the end of 1942. In the meantime, the 90/53 were installed on the Lancia 3RO and Breda 51 trucks, as well as being used to arm

30 self-propelled vehicles on the hull of the M41 tank. In anti-aircraft fire it was associated with Gamma and BGS fire stations. The 90/53 cannon was used above all for the anti-aircraft and coastal defense of the national territory, the autocannoni operated in Libya, Tunisia, southern France and Sicily, the self-propelled in Sicily. After 8 September, production continued for the needs of the German Armed Forces, which used the cannon in Italy and Germany, with the denomination of 9.0 cm. Flak-41 (i). The 90/53 cannon turned out to be an excellent firearm, with ballistic characteristics superior to the German 88/55, a true multi-role weapon capable of operating in anti-aircraft, counter-tank, anti-landing, anti-ship and land targets. Unfortunately, the lack of firing centers, radar, high-powered photoelectrics, the scarce supply of ammunition and mechanical timed fuses, negated the excellent performance of this excellent firearm, which remained supplied to the Army and to the Navy until the 1960s. The first trucks set up on heavy trucks were criticized for the excessively high silhouette for use in desert territory, the poor mobility on varied terrain, the long transition times from towing to firing configuration.

Technical data 90/53 gun
Piece weight in battery: 6.240 kg
Vertical shooting sector: -2° +85°
Horizontal shooting sector: 360°
Grenade weight: 10.1 kg
Initial speed: 850 m/s
Maximum range: 17,4 km – 12 km c.a.

In the Armed Forces of the R.S.I. the 90/53 gun was used by the following units:
- Ar.Co. :
    - 1st Group "Amerio": (?) Batteries - (?) pieces
    - 2nd Group "Frattini": 4 Batteries - 16 pieces
    - 3rd Group "Gambassini": 4 Batteries - 16 pieces
    - 4th Group "Cavalli": 4 Batteries - 16 pieces
    - 5th Group" Lattanti": 4 Batteries - 16 pieces
    - 6th Group "Paganuzzi": 4 Batteries - 16 pieces
- "Decima" Navy Infantry Division: "Condottieri" Artillery Regiment - "Colleoni" Artillery Group: 1 autocannone
- 1st "Etna" Anti-Parachute and Anti-Aircraft Division - G.N.R .: (?) Pieces
- 1114th Heavy Artillery Group (France) - 3 Battery: 12 pieces
- 1st Coastal Position Artillery Group - 2nd Battery: 4 pieces
- 2nd Coastal Position Artillery Group - 5th Battery: 4 pieces
- 9th Artillery Group Coastal Position - 4 Battery (?) 16 pieces
- 11th Artillery Group Coastal Position - (?) Battery (?) Pieces
- Coastal Position Artillery Group "Gruppo Pezzini" - FB 16: 4 pieces

Note
A total of 28 gun batteries of various calibers were present in the Recruiting Center, at the Training Corps and in the Deposits of the Ar.Co.

FOREIGN ARTILLERY

20/65 Flak 30–38, FLAKVIERLING

Produced by Rheinmetall-Borsig, the Flak-30 was adopted by the Kriegsmarine in 1934 and by the Luftwaffe in '35. It derives from the 2 cm MG C / 30L machine gun of naval origin adopted by the Reichswerhr in 1931. It was characterized by a single platform carriage used indifferently in fixed or mobile positions, by a complicated electro-optical aiming mechanism and was powered by a tank per box of 20 shots. The main defects were: the high weight of the carriage, the low rate of fire, the low speed in swing and tappet. Mauser was in charge of the modifications that led to the creation of the Flak 38 in 1939/40. In the Royal Army the first 20/65 Flak were obtained following the occupation of Greece, subsequently Germany delivered dozens of pieces of both models. It was used in territorial anti-aircraft defense in Italy, the Aegean and Greece.

To further increase the volume of fire and compensate for the low destructive power, a Flakvierling Flak-38 quadruple carriage was adopted. This complex was also introduced into the Royal Army in a few dozen specimens. In addition to the Royal Army, the Royal Navy also introduced the quadruple German machine gun to arm the smaller ships. In November 1943, Viberti installed a single Flak-38 on the AS43 vehicle, 13 units were built for the German exploration departments.

Technical data 20/65 machine gun
Piece weight in battery: 470 kg   (according to other sources 412kg)
Vertical shooting sector: -10° +90°   (according to other sources -20°+90°)
Horizontal shooting sector: 360°
Grenade weight: 115 gr
Initial speed: 900 m/s
Maximum range: 4,8 km – 3,8 km a.a.

In the Armed Forces of the R.S.I. the 20/65 Flak 30 and Flak 38 machine gunners were employed by the following units:
- Ar.Co .: (?) Batteries (?) Pieces

20/70 Oerlikon Machine Gun

Arma paragonabile al modello Breda, era caratterizzata da un affusto dotato di ruote di grande diametro trainabile da un automezzo leggero. Era impiegabile sia per il tiro contraereo che terrestre, su ruote o su treppiede. Su affusto a candeliere era destinata all'impiego fisso, a bordo e a terra. Venne introdotto nel 1940 acquistando esemplari sia campali che da posizione. Nel modello campale era in dotazione alle unità da sbarco della Regia Marina e delle Camicie Nere Speciali.

Technical data 20/70 machine gun
Piece weight in battery: 247/291/363 kg depending on the model

Vertical shooting sector: -15° +85°
Horizontal shooting sector   : 360°
Grenade weight: 126 gr
Initial speed: 830 m/s
Maximum range: 5 km – 3,7 km a.a.

In the Armed Forces of the R.S.I. the 20/70 machine gun was used by the following units:
- Ar.Co .: (?) Batteries (?) Pieces

Flak-18 da 8,8 cm gun

Secretly studied by German technicians sent to Sweden to evade the clauses of the Treaty of Versailles, in 1933, with the advent of National Socialism, it was immediately put into production at Krupp. Piece with excellent ballistic characteristics ensured by a long gun muzzle and a very perfected ammunition, it was extremely mobile thanks to the 2-axle trolley with elastic suspension pulled by a half-track tractor, it was also equipped with very advanced aiming tools that allowed shooting direct and indirect, with the weapon enslaved to the Zeiss firing unit. Since the baptism of fire in Spain, it proved to be a deadly counter-tank weapon, capable of knocking out all tanks in service. Two other improved versions were derived from the Flak-18: the Flak-36 and the Flak-37. It was built in more than 10.000 units until the end of the conflict, it was used to arm armored vehicles, railway carriages, light ships, coastal posts, in addition to the natural use of anti-aircraft weapons. In the Royal Army, the first 88/55 entered service in 1940, partly deployed in North Africa and partly assigned to MACA. In 1943 there were over 100 batteries in service, some of which were slaved to radar. It was used in North Africa, Tunisia, Greece, the Aegean, Italy. Only in Libya and Tunisia the 88/55 was used by the Royal Army also in anti-tank function.

Technical data 88/55 gun
Piece weight in battery: 5.500 kg
Vertical shooting sector: -3° +85°
Horizontal shooting sector: 360°
Grenade weight: 9,1 kg
Initial speed: 820 m/s
Maximum range: 14,8 km – 10,6 km a.a.

In the Armed Forces of the R.S.I. the 88/55 gun was used by the following units:
- 1st "Etna" Anti-Parachute and Anti-Aircraft Division - G.N.R .: (?) Pieces

▲ Breda 20/65 machine gun model 35, located on an elevated platform, used by the 5th Regiment of the Territorial Defense Militia in Istria (Arena Archive).

▼ Alpini of the "Tagliamento" Alpine Regiment at Chiesa San Giorgio with a 20/65 Breda machine gun (Archive of the "Tagliamento" Alpine Regiment).

▲ Alpini of the "Monterosa" Division in a position on the Ligurian coast equipped with a fixed 20/65 machine gun ("Monterosa" Archive).

▲ Curious position in the rear of the Gothic Line, equipped with a 20/65 machine gun of the "Etna" G.N.R. Division, disguised so as to appear a haystack (Viziano Archive).

▼ 20/65 machine gun of the "Alberto da Giussano" Artillery Group of the "Decima" Division on the Gothic Line, put in battery in a pit camouflaged with makeshift vehicles (Panzarasa Archive).

▲ The servants of this Breda 20/65 of the Decima find themselves operating in really difficult climatic and environmental conditions (Arena Archive).

▼ Before leaving for the Senio front, the "Lupo" Battalion of the "Decima" Division parades in full warfare through the streets of Milan (Crippa Archive).

▲ The "Lupo" of the X MAS was equipped with 4 Breda 20/65 anti-aircraft machine guns, very useful for defending their units, especially on the Senio, where they were easy targets of the enemy air force (Crippa Archive).

▼ Station equipped with a 20/65 machine gun of the "Mussolini" Bersaglieri Battalion in Piedicolle (Francesconi Archive).

▲ 20 mm machine gun of the Black Brigade of Turin "Capelli", photographed during a Mass at the camp (Monti - Satiz).

▼ Arditi of Legione "Ettore Muti from Milan, photographed in Piedmont with a 20/65 machine gun (Sandri Archive).

▲ At least two Alfa Romeo 430 trucks of the "Muti" Legion, a unit of Arditi included in the Republican Police, had been equipped with Scotti-Isotta Fraschini-O.M anti-aircraft machine guns 20/70 (Sandri Archive).

▼ Close-up of a Scotti-Isotta Fraschini-O.M. machine gun 20/70 on candlestick carriage, installed on Alfa Romeo 430, of the "Ettore Muti" Mobile Autonomous Legion, filmed during the parade held on December 17, 1944 in Milan on the occasion of Mussolini's visit (Sandri Archive).

▲ Armored trolley armed with Scotti machine gun of the "Muti" Legion captured in Milan by the partisans during the insurrection of 25th April (Archivio Crippa).

▼ Scotti machine gun in a fixed position served by airmen from an Anti-Parachute Battalion of the Republican National Air Force. The military use helmets with the Army Republican eagle, a common practice among the soldiers of the Anti-Parachute Battalions (Crippa).

▲ Some Scotti machine guns of the "Muti" were pulled by small FIAT 508 trucks (Crippa Archive).

▲ Airmen of the VII Anti-Paratrooper Battalion defending an airport in the Bergamo area, with a Scotti 20mm anti-aircraft machine gun (Arena Archive).

▲ Anti-aircraft post armed with Scotti machine guns in an airport in Northern Italy (Crippa Archive).

▼ Scotti-Isotta Fraschini machine gun - O.M. from 20/70 in service in an Ar.Co anti-aircraft battery (Arena Archive).

▲ Servant of a twin Breda 37/54 machine gun of the Ar.Co. (Arena Archive).

▼ 76/40 gun supplied by an anti-aircraft artillery group of the Ar.Co. (Arena Archive).

▲ 76/40 anti-aircraft gun used by the IX Coastal Position Artillery Group (Arena Archive).

▲ Airmen of the Co. used in a mixed battery equipped with 76 mm anti-aircraft guns. The truck is an Italian Lancia 3RO (Arena Archive).

▲ Artillerymen of the Ar.Co. during an air attack. During the R.S.I., the anti-aircraft artillery was assigned to the Republican National Air Force (Arena Archive).

▼ Mussolini in sight of a department of the Ar.Co. in August 1944: in the center of the image a 90/53 anti-aircraft gun (Pisanò Archive).

▲ 90/53 gun of the "Amerio" Group I of the Ar.Co. (Arena Archive).

▲ Artillerymen intent on loading a 90/53 gun in service in an Ar.Co Group (Arena Archive).

▼ Antiaircraft gun from 90/53 of the Ar.Co. ready to set fire (Arena Archive).

▲ Servants of a 90/53 anti-aircraft piece of the Ar.Co. they scan the sky in search of enemy planes (Arena Archive).

▼ Battery of 90/53 guns of the Ar.Co. (Arena Archive).

▲ The barrel of this 90/53 gun of the Ar.Co. it is at maximum elevation, pointed towards the sky, ready to fire at enemy aircraft (Arena Archive).

▲ This image allows you to appreciate the arrangement of the pieces of an Ar.Co. Battery, while in the foreground you can see an operator who, through the radio, can quickly distribute the shooting coordinates to all the pieces (Arena Archive).

▼ Young legionaries of the "Etna" Division of the Republican National Guard during an air attack in the last days of the war (Arena Archive).

▲ Personnel of a mixed Italian-German anti-aircraft battery maneuver a 20/65 Flak 38 machine gun (Pisanò Archive).

▼ Airmen of the Social Republic framed in the 4th Battery of the 331st Flak Group with an 88/54 anti-aircraft gun. This Battery, located in Ghedi (BS), was made up exclusively of young Lombard people (Pisanò Archive).

▲ 8.8 cm Flak-18 cannon in service at the IX Autonomous Company of the "Etna" Division of the G.N.R. in Bagnolo S. Vito (MN), on the Gothic Line (Archivio Giusto).

▲ Legionary of "Etna" maneuvers a Flak-18 cannon in Correggio Micheli (MN). The "Etna" Division was a large unit of the Republican National Guard, formed by bringing together the previously autonomous anti-aircraft and anti-parachute units (Archivio Giusto).

▲ Young legionaries of the "Etna" Division with an 8.8 cm anti-aircraft gun (Pisanò Archive).

CONCLUSIONS

Speaking of conclusion, when it comes to the Armed Forces of CSR, is always at least risky, the lack of information and documentation, the disappearance of the historical diaries of the Departments, the difficulty in finding veterans available to tell their story, undoubtedly creates considerable difficulty in finding reliable data to verify and publish. The transcribed data therefore refer only to those of which there is certainty, even if as can be seen in many cases they are incomplete. Despite this, we still wanted to indicate at least the Department in which the artillery pieces in question were certainly present, in order to allow enthusiasts to be able to carry out further research on the matter.

▲ Servants of an 88 gun of the "Etna" Division in a moment of rest. As they belonged to the Republican National Guard, the "Etna" gunners wore the black shirt, like all the other legionaries (Arena Archive).

BIBLIOGRAPHY

BOOKS
- Arena Nino, "L'Italia in Guerra 1940/45", Albertelli Editore, 1997.
- Arena Nino, "R.S.I. Forze Armate della Repubblica Sociale Italiana", volumi I – II – III, Albertelli Editore
- Arena Nino, "Soli contro Tutti", Edizioni Ultima Crociata, 1993.
- Associazione Reduci Reggimento Alpini "Tagliamento", "Reggimento Alpini "Tagliamento", stampato in proprio.
- Baldrati Pieramedeo, "San Marco... San Marco, Storia di una Divisione", stampato in proprio, 1989.
- Bonvicini Guido, "Decima Marinai! Decima Comandante!", Mursia, 1988.
- Cappellano Filippo, "Le Artiglierie del Regio Esercito", Storia Militare, 1998.
- Corbanese Girolamo, Mansutti Aldo, "Storia d'Italia - Zona di Operazioni del Litorale Adriatico - I Protagonisti (settembre 1943 – maggio 1945)", Aviani & Aviani editori, 2008.
- Cornia Carlo, "MONTEROSA - Storia della Divisione Alpina Monterosa", Del Bianco Editore, 1971.
- Crippa Paolo, "I carristi di Mussolini - Il Gruppo corazzato "Leonessa" dalla M.V.S.N. alla R.S.I., " Soldiershop Publishing, 2019.
- Cucut Carlo, "Alpini nella città di Fiume 1944 – 1945", Marvia Edizioni, 2012.
- Cucut Carlo, "Le forze armate della RSI 1943 – 1945 - Forze di terra", Gruppo Modellistico Trentino, 2005.
- Cucut Carlo, "Penne Nere sul confine orientale - Storia del Reggimento Alpini "Tagliamento" 1943 – 1945", Marvia Edizioni, 2008.
- Cucut Carlo, Bobbio Roberto, "Attilio Viziano - Ricordi di un corrispondente di guerra", Marvia Edizioni, 2008.
- Cucut Carlo, Crippa Paolo, " Reparti Alpini nella R.S.I." Soldiershop Publishing, 2019.
- Cucut Carlo, Crippa Paolo, "I reparti controguerriglia della R.S.I.", Marvia Edizioni, 2020.
- Cucut Carlo, Crippa Paolo, "Reparti Bersaglieri nella R.S.I.", Soldiershop Publishing, 2019.
- Cucut Carlo, Crippa Paolo, "Le divisioni dell'E.N.R. 1943 -1945", volume 1, Soldiershop Publishing, 2020.
- Cucut Carlo, Crippa Paolo, "Milizia Difesa Territoriale e Guardie Civiche nell'O.Z.A.K. 1943 -1945", Soldiershop Publishing, 2020.
- De Lazzari Primo, "Le SS Italiane", Teti Editore, 2002.
- Fiaschi Cesare, "Un Alpino dal Regio Esercito alla R.S.I.", Editrice Lo Scarabeo, 2005.
- Francesconi Teodoro, "Bersaglieri in Venezia Giulia 1943/1945, Casa Editrice del Baccia, 1969.
- Gamberini Maurizio, Maculan Riccardo, "Battaglione Fulmine Xa Flottiglia Mas 1944/1945", Editrice Lo Scarabeo, 1994.
- Giusto Michele, "L'Ultima frontiera dell'Onore Fiamme Bianche al fronte - IX Compagnia Autonoma Cacciatori di Cacc. Carri - Divisione "Etna" G.N.R.", NovAntico Editore, 2001.
- Kuchler Heinz, "Fregi, Mostrine e Distintivi della R.S.I.", Intergest, 1974.
- La Serra Raffaele, "Il Battaglione Guastatori Alpini Valanga", 1999.
- Mengoli Silvia, "Una Valle un Reggimento 1944/1945 il 4° Alpini in Valle d'Aosta", Editrice Lo Scarabeo, 1997.
- Occhi Roberto, "Siam Fatti Così! Storia della Legione Mobile Ettore Muti", Ritter Edizioni, 2002.
- Perissinotto Marino, "Duri a Morire - Storia del Battaglione di Fanteria di Marina "Barbarigo", Albertelli Editore, 1997.
- Perissinotto Marino, Panzarasa Carlo Alfredo, "Come la Fenice - Storia del Gruppo Artiglieria "San

Giorgio" nella Decima Mas", Editoriale Lupo, 2003.
• Pignato Nicola, "Le Armi della Fanteria Italiana nella Seconda Guerra Mondiale",Albertelli Editore, 1978.
• Pignato Nicola, Cappellano Filippo, "   Dal TL 37 all'AS 43", Gruppo Modellistico Trentino, 1997.
• Pisanò Giorgio, "Storia delle Forze Armate della Repubblica Sociale Italiana", C.D.L. Edizioni, 1993.
• Stabile Tommaso, Borgatti Elvezio, "Gruppo Corazzato "M" Leonessa 1943/1945", Associazione Reduci Gruppo Corazzato "Leonessa"stampato in proprio.
• Ufficiali II Gruppo/2° Reggimento Artiglieria della Divisione "Littorio", " L'ultima difesa 1945", stampato in proprio, 1992.

MAGAZINES
• "Historica Nuova" - Centro Studi di Storia Contemporanea
• "Eserciti e Armi"
• "Guerra Civile"
• "Milites"
• "Panorama Difesa"
• "R.I.D. - Rivista Italiana Difesa"
• "Raids"
• "Rivista Militare"
• "Rivista Storica"
• "SGM - Seconda Guerra Mondiale"
• "Storia del Novecento"
• "Storia del XX Secolo"
• "Storia Militare"
• "Storie & Battaglie"
• "Uniformi e Armi"
• Notiziario "Cjossul" - Associazione Reduci Reggimento Alpini Tagliamento
• Notiziario "Monterosa" - Associazione Reduci Divisione Alpina Monterosa
• Notiziario "Tagliamento" - Associazione Reduci Reggimento Alpini Tagliamento
• Notiziario "ACTA" - Istituto Storico della RSI

TITOLI GIÀ PUBBLICATI
TITLES ALREADY PUBLISHING

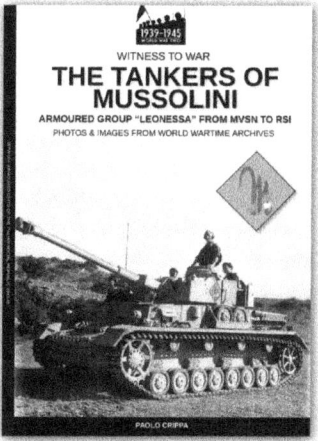
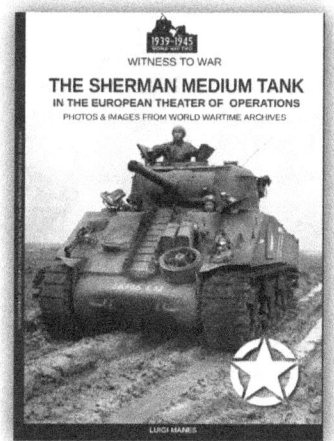

www.ingramcontent.com/pod-product-compliance
Lightning Source LLC
LaVergne TN
LVHW081545070526
838199LV00057B/3783